150 Quotes to Break the Chains of Debt

Timeless Insights on Mastering Leverage and
Securing Financial Freedom

M. Angelo Hunter

150 Quotes to Break the Chains of Debt: Timeless Insights on Mastering Leverage and Securing Financial Freedom

Published by Michael Angelo Hunter

How to Use This Book

This book provides a toolkit for transforming your perspective on debt, whether you aim to escape its hold or leverage it to build wealth. To maximize these insights, begin by identifying the areas of your financial life where you feel stuck or uncertain. Let each quote serve as a reflection, and see if they can reshape how you think about debt and leverage. Take time to reflect on the meaning of each quote, analyzing how its principles can be applied to your decisions, whether small everyday choices or larger investment strategies. Whether you read one or two quotes daily or read the entire book in a single sitting, the goal is to combine these timeless principles with actionable steps. By doing so, you'll develop a clearer, more strategic mindset about debt, empowering you to turn liabilities into opportunities for growth and lasting financial freedom. Good luck on your journey, and thank you for reading.

- M. Angelo Hunter

1) *"There are three ways a smart person can go broke: liquor, ladies, and leverage."*

— Charlie Munger

Charlie gives us a memorable warning about the dangers of losing control in both personal and financial matters. When he mentions "liquor," Munger isn't simply referring to alcohol but to the broader concept of addiction and escapism. Overindulgence in vices can cloud judgment, drain resources, and lead to poor decisions, which can be catastrophic in business and investing. Clear thinking is essential, and when compromised, it opens the door to bad choices that can lead to financial ruin. "Ladies" refers to the distractions of relationships and lifestyle inflation, particularly when people chase high-cost endeavors to impress others. This pursuit of status or fleeting pleasures can divert attention and energy away from long-term financial goals, causing wasteful spending. Finally, "leverage" refers to using borrowed money to invest, which can amplify gains and losses. While leverage can accelerate wealth creation, it also dramatically increases risk. If the market turns against you, debt can magnify losses, leading to insolvency. Munger's warning highlights the importance of balance, self-discipline, and caution. Careless living and reckless financial behavior, whether through addiction, distractions, or excessive borrowing, can easily destroy even substantial wealth. The key lesson is to stay grounded and exercise control in all areas of life, especially when dealing with money.

2) "Leverage is the reason some people become rich and others do not become rich."

— Robert Kiyosaki

Leverage is a financial strategy that involves using borrowed capital to increase the potential return on investment, thereby amplifying the investor's buying power and potential profits. In otherwords, using borrowed money to invest.

In the context of real estate, for example, an investor might make a 20% down payment on a property (using their own capital) and finance the remaining 80% through a mortgage (debt). This means they control the entire asset while only needing 20% of its value in cash. The impact of leverage on the investor's return, called Return on Equity (ROE) is significant. It can dramatically increase the returns earned on the investor's initial capital. Using borrowed funds amplifies the investor's ROE because they earn returns on the total value of the property, not just their initial investment. A 10% increase in the value of the property results in a 50% increase in the investor's initial equity. However, while leverage can accelerate wealth creation by enhancing ROE, it also introduces greater risk, as it can magnify losses if the investment drops and obligates the investor to meet debt repayments regardless of the investment's performance. It only takes a 20% drawdown to the property's value to wipe out the investor's initial equity.

It's like using a lever to lift a heavy object. You can achieve much more with less effort. However, leverage is a double-edged sword; it can amplify gains but magnify losses. Understanding how to use leverage wisely can be the difference between building wealth and falling into debt. Educate yourself on investment strategies, assess risks carefully, and consider how leveraging resources, money, time, or skills can help you achieve your financial goals.

3) "A man in debt is so far a slave."

— Ralph Waldo Emerson

Historically, debts could lead to literal servitude; today, they can imprison us in jobs we dislike or lifestyles that don't fulfill us. Consider how financial obligations may be dictating your life's choices. What steps can you take to lighten the load and move more freely toward your aspirations?

True freedom comes from within. Debt is a self-imposed shackle that limits our potential. It's like navigating life with an anchor dragging behind us; every step requires more effort, and progress is slowed. Compound interest works against us rather than for us, the most pernicious anchor of them all, one that grows with time.

4) "Never spend your money before you have earned it."

— Thomas Jefferson

Though he ultimately amassed wealth, Thomas Jefferson, the third President of the United States, was no stranger to financial hardship. His advice reflects lessons learned from personal experience. Jefferson himself struggled with debt throughout his life. Despite being a wealthy landowner and third President of the United States, he faced significant financial difficulties, partly due to his lifestyle and the debts inherited from his father-in-law. His personal experiences with debt, including the sale of his property after his death to settle outstanding balances, make this advice particularly poignant. It serves as a cautionary tale, suggesting that even those with wealth and status can fall into financial trouble if they spend recklessly.

Spending money before you've earned it is like building a house on sand. It is unstable and risky. Spending before earning is a behavior that can trap you in a cycle of debt. By embracing patience and financial discipline, you can avoid unnecessary debt and foster a sense of accomplishment and security. So, the next time you're tempted to make an advance purchase, pause and consider waiting until you've earned the means.

Today, it is easier than ever to spend before you earn. Nearly everyone has access to credit card debt or buy now pay later services. Be wary of taking this credit because it will add up faster than you can earn and overtake you with an avalanche of interest.

5) *"Beware of little expenses; a small leak will sink a great ship."*

— Benjamin Franklin

Benjamin Franklin, a man of wisdom and practicality, compares minor, unchecked expenses to tiny leaks in a ship's hull. At first glance, they seem insignificant, but they can lead to disastrous consequences over time. It's reminiscent of the saying, "Death by a thousand cuts." or "The straw that broke the camel's back."

Small daily indulgences, like premium coffee or subscription services, can add up, draining resources that could be directed toward more meaningful goals. Try tracking your expenditures for a month; you might be surprised by how the little things accumulate. Plugging these leaks can keep your financial ship steady and on course and get your wealth snowball rolling in the right direction.

6) "Debt is like any other trap, easy enough to get into, but hard enough to get out of."

— Henry Wheeler Shaw

Acquiring debt is deceptively easy. Modern financial institutions have strong incentives to extend credit: if they believe you can repay or can seize your assets if you don't, they want you to take on debt. They will profit from the interest on the money they lend you.

Taking on debt can be likened to wandering into a maze: it is easy to enter, but finding the exit becomes a complex challenge. Credit cards, loans, and easy financing options give us immediate gratification, masking the long-term commitment required to repay them. Before accepting offers to increase your credit, ask yourself: are these opportunities or traps? Before borrowing, educate yourself on the terms and consider the future implications before stepping in. You may be signing up for something your future self will regret.

7) "He who takes a loan gets sorrow."

— Traditional Russian Proverb

This proverb succinctly captures the emotional burden that often accompanies borrowing. Taking a loan might solve an immediate problem, but it can introduce ongoing stress and worry, like inviting a guest who overstays their welcome. The sorrow stems from the obligation and the potential strain on personal relationships and well-being. Before taking on new debt, weigh the temporary relief against the long-term emotional cost. Can alternative solutions alleviate your needs without adding to your burdens? What type of debt are you taking on? Will your debt increase your income or revenue, or must you trade your life to service it? Avoid debt that requires you to trade your life.

8) "Rather go to bed without dinner than rise in debt."

— Benjamin Franklin

Franklin's advice emphasizes the value of sacrifice for long-term stability. Skipping a meal is a temporary discomfort, but debt can become a persistent thorn in one's side. It's akin to fasting to cleanse the body and short-term deprivation for greater health benefits. Franklin's perspective encourages us to prioritize financial health over immediate gratification. Before you buy something, ask yourself if it is a need versus a want. If it is only a want, never go into debt for it.

9) "The man who never has money enough to pay his debts has too much of something else."

— James Lendall Basford

Chronic debt may be a symptom of excess in other areas, such as spending habits, material possessions, or even pride. Like a body with too many parasites, this imbalance hinders the ability to grow healthy. Self-reflection can reveal the underlying issues contributing to financial strain. It may be time to declutter not just our living spaces but also our expenditures. Simplifying our lifestyles might free up resources to settle debts and bring a sense of balance and contentment. Never try to keep up with the Neighbours because they are likely over-consuming, and they will drag you down with them.

10) "Debt is like a poison - it can slowly eat away at your soul if you're not careful."

— Metaphorical Expression

When unmanaged, debt can have a corrosive effect on your spirit and outlook on life. It's like a slow-acting toxin that accumulates over time, subtly impacting your health before symptoms become apparent. The stress and anxiety associated with mounting debt can strain relationships, diminish productivity, and erode self-esteem. Acknowledging the problem is the first antidote. Seek support through financial counseling, trusted friends, or educational resources. Remember, taking proactive steps can neutralize the poison and restore vitality to your life.

11) *"The more debt we accumulate, the less money we have to invest in our future."*

— Kevin McCarthy

There is a significant opportunity cost associated with paying interest on debt. Every dollar spent on interest is not invested in assets, education, retirement, or personal growth; it's like dead money not captured on the balance sheet. Consider that debt on the balance sheet works against you through interest payments, increasing your costs. By reducing debt and minimizing interest payments, we can redirect funds toward investments that yield long-term benefits, compounding over time like a seed growing into a flourishing tree. Less debt means less risk and more cash flow into your pocket.

12) *"Debt is the shadow of the wealth you desire but cannot afford."*

— Proverb

Debt is a deceptive reflection, an illusion of wealth without substance. Building on top of debt is like chasing a mirage in the desert; the closer you think you get, the further it recedes, leaving you dehydrated and unfulfilled. Acquiring items through debt may offer temporary satisfaction but doesn't equate to true wealth. Instead, it can lead to a cycle of longing and indebtedness. Consider redefining your perception of wealth. Is it possible to find contentment in what you have or to set realistic goals for acquiring what you desire without falling into debt? Wealth is something you cannot see in many cases.

13) *"An investment in knowledge always pays the best interest."*

— Benjamin Franklin

In a world where markets fluctuate and material possessions depreciate, knowledge is a timeless asset. Education and skills development enhance your earning potential and adaptability, providing returns that compound over a lifetime. Consider allocating resources toward learning, whether formal education, groups, self-study, or your own longshot projects. This investment can open doors to opportunities that might otherwise remain closed, and it is hard to predict how much the knowledge you cultivate will compound over time.

14) "Using other people's money is the smartest way to leverage your own."

— Robert Kiyosaki

Use other people's money (OPM) to build wealth. By leveraging borrowed funds for income-generating investments, you can amplify your financial growth without solely relying on your capital. It's akin to planting seeds in a garden you didn't have to buy; you reap the harvest while minimizing your initial outlay. However, this approach requires careful planning and risk management. Ensure that any debt incurred is "good debt" and used for assets that appreciate or generate income, not for depreciating assets or consumables. Educate yourself on financial instruments and strategies to make informed decisions using leverage. Only use OPM if you know you are buying a sound asset, as your reputation will generate more wealth than any single deal.

15) "Neither a borrower nor a lender be; for loan oft loses both itself and friend."

— William Shakespeare

There are risks when mixing finances with personal relationships. Lending or borrowing money among friends can introduce tension and resentment, much like a discordant note in a harmonious melody. The potential loss extends beyond the money to the friendship itself. Before entering such arrangements, consider the value of the relationship and whether it's worth jeopardizing. If lending is unavoidable, treat it as a gift without expectations to preserve goodwill. People cannot often mix friendship or family with business or financial affairs.

16) "The chains of habit are too light to be felt until they are too heavy to be broken."

— Warren Buffett

One of the most successful investors of all time, Warren Buffett, underscores the subtlety with which habit, financial or otherwise, becomes ingrained. Early on, spending habits might seem inconsequential, like threads easily snapped. Over time, they intertwine into unbreakable ropes that bind us. This metaphor serves as a caution to cultivate positive habits while they are still malleable. Regular saving, prudent investing, and mindful spending can set you on a path to financial freedom before detrimental habits take hold. Always invest and save before you're lesson self can trick you into spending your hard-earned capital.

17) "Debt is the devil's net cast wide to catch all who lust after more than they can earn."

— Old English Saying

This vivid metaphor portrays debt as a trap set for those driven by excessive desire. It's reminiscent of tales where characters make deals with the devil, seeking immediate gains without considering the ultimate cost. The devil feeds off instant gratification, luxuries, status symbols, or experiences beyond one's means. Recognizing this temptation allows us to pause and assess our true needs versus wants. Cultivating gratitude for what we have and setting realistic goals can help us avoid entanglement in debt's net. Avoid making this particular deal with the devil.

18) *"The worst bankruptcy in the world is the person who has lost his enthusiasm. "*

— H.W. Arnold

While not directly related to financial debt, this quote speaks to a deeper form of impoverishment, the loss of spirit and motivation. It's like a well without water, outwardly intact but lacking its essential purpose. Financial struggles can contribute to this state, draining energy and hope. However, maintaining enthusiasm can be a powerful asset in overcoming challenges. It's the fuel that drives innovation, resilience, and recovery. Surround yourself with supportive people, engage in activities that inspire you, and remember that setbacks are temporary on the path to success. You cannot succeed without failure.

19) "You can't live forever off the bank's money."

— Dan Peña

Dan Peña, known as the "Trillion Dollar Man," offers a blunt reminder that relying on borrowed funds is unsustainable. Living on credit creates an illusion of wealth that doesn't reflect true financial health. By developing multiple streams of income, focusing on wealth creation rather than consumption, and practicing fiscal responsibility, you can build a solid foundation that doesn't depend on external support.

20) *"Debt keeps you tethered to yesterday's misfortunes."*

— Warren Buffett

Imagine trying to walk forward while a rope pulls you back. This is how debt anchors us to past decisions. It prevents us from fully embracing new opportunities, much like a ship anchored in a harbor unable to set sail. Acknowledging this rope is the first step toward releasing it. Consider consolidating debts, creating a realistic repayment plan, or seeking professional advice. By addressing the debt, you free yourself to focus on the present and future, unburdened by the weight of yesterday. If you're too indebted, you have no room on your balance sheet to take advantage of a new opportunity. You are not prepared for good fortune when you are overly indebted.

21) "A promise made is a debt unpaid."

— Robert W. Service

Consider a promise as a handshake of the soul, an unspoken contract that binds us morally. Robert W. Service highlights that a commitment, once given, carries the weight of debt until fulfilled. When you make a promise, the responsibility remains yours to complete it. Breaking a promise diminishes trust and can burden you with guilt. Reflect on the promises you've made. Are there any awaiting fulfillment? Taking steps to honor them can nurture relationships and reinforce your integrity.

22) "To preserve their independence, we must not let our rulers load us with perpetual debt. We must make our election between economy and liberty, or profusion and servitude."

— Thomas Jefferson

There is a subtle erosion of freedom through mounting national debt. It's akin to a frog in gradually heating water, unaware of the danger until it's too late. By choosing economy over extravagance, both nations and individuals safeguard their independence. This perspective invites us to consider how our financial choices affect our autonomy. Are we, through unchecked spending, willingly exchanging liberty for temporary comforts? Embracing fiscal responsibility can be a step toward preserving the freedoms we cherish.

As of 2023, the mounting national debt in the United States has reached unprecedented levels, surpassing $31 trillion. This escalating debt results from persistent budget deficits, where government spending exceeds revenue. Contributing factors include increased expenditures on social programs, defense, and interest payments on existing debt, combined with tax policies that have yet to keep pace with spending. The growing national debt poses significant challenges, such as higher interest costs that can strain future budgets, potential impacts on economic growth, and concerns about long-term fiscal sustainability. The nation slowly goes broke, and thus, its citizens' quality of life erodes.

23) "Smart borrowing can be part of a successful financial plan."

— Dave Ramsey

Dave Ramsey, a personal finance expert famous for advocating a no-debt approach, acknowledges that not all debt is detrimental. When used wisely, borrowing can be a strategic tool to achieve significant goals like buying a home or investing in buissness. It's like using a ladder to reach a higher place, you still need to climb carefully. The key is to differentiate between "good debt" and "bad debt." Good debt has the potential to increase your net worth or enhance your life in meaningful ways. Good debt buys an asset that earns you income after paying all the interest, like a rental property or a helpful piece of equipment. Before taking on debt, assess whether it aligns with your financial objectives and whether you have a clear plan for repayment.

24) "Creditors have better memories than debtors."

— Benjamin Franklin

Those who owe money seldom forget, while those who owe might prefer to let it slip their minds. It's like the relationship between the sun and the shadow: the creditor remains ever-present, casting a constant reminder, while the debtor hopes to escape notice. This dynamic can strain relationships and create tension. It's wise to address debts proactively to maintain harmony and uphold credibility. By setting reminders or establishing a repayment plan, you can ensure commitments are met, fostering trust and mutual respect.

25) "Blessed are the young, for they shall inherit the national debt."

— Herbert Hoover

The national debt is passed onto future generations. It's reminiscent of inheriting an old house with hidden structural issues or a business with unexpected burdens that hamper progress. This quote serves as a reminder of our collective responsibility to manage resources wisely. On a personal level, consider the financial habits and values we impart to the younger generation. Are we setting them up for success or saddling them with undue burdens? When voting, consider which party will act the most fiscally responsible, although that is becoming less and less common as Western societies age. If your country is in debt, you as an individual certainly don't want to be.

26) "Running into debt isn't so bad. It's running into creditors that hurts."

— Kin Hubbard

While acquiring debt may seem painless, the real discomfort arises when repayment is due. It's like enjoying a feast without considering the impending indigestion. This analogy underscores the importance of foresight and planning. Before taking on debt, envision the full journey, not just the initial gratification but also the responsibility that follows. Such mindfulness can prevent unpleasant surprises and promote healthier financial choices.

27) "Interest on debts grows without rain."

— Yiddish Proverb

This proverb cleverly illustrates how interest accumulates effortlessly, much like weeds overtaking a garden without care. It's a silent growth that can overwhelm if left unchecked. Just as a diligent gardener regularly tends to their plants, we must actively manage debts to prevent them from spiraling. Reviewing interest rates, consolidating loans, or increasing payments can mitigate this relentless growth. Taking proactive steps can keep your financial garden flourishing.

28) "A small debt produces a debtor; a large one, an enemy."

— Publilius Syrus

The is an escalating tension that comes with increasing debt. A minor obligation might strain a relationship, but substantial debt can sever it entirely, turning friends into foes—much like a crack in a mirror that spreads until the reflection is unrecognizable. Renowned investor Ray Dalio echoes this sentiment by emphasizing the dangers of excessive debt. He points out that accumulating debt beyond one's capacity to repay not only leads to personal financial crises but can also erode trust and damage relationships. Dalio advocates for understanding the implications of debt cycles and stresses the importance of maintaining a balance between borrowing and one's ability to fulfill obligations. To preserve relationships, it's crucial to communicate openly about financial matters and approach borrowing with caution. Honesty and clarity can prevent misunderstandings and maintain trust.

29) "Wealth consists not in having great possessions, but in having few wants."

— Epictetus

Epictetus, a Stoic philosopher, teaches that true wealth is found in contentment. It's like a calm lake undisturbed by external forces. By reducing our desires, we free ourselves from the pursuit of material excess and the debt that often accompanies it. This perspective invites introspection: what do we truly need to be happy? Embracing simplicity can lead to a richer, more fulfilling life untethered by unnecessary obligations.

30) *"A man who pays his bills on time is soon forgotten."*

— Oscar Wilde

With his characteristic wit, Oscar Wilde suggests that reliability doesn't garner attention. It's like a smoothly running engine, often unnoticed until it falters. While this might seem discouraging, there's value in the peace and stability that come with financial responsibility. Paying bills on time may not bring accolades, but it builds a solid foundation for trust and credibility. Consider it a quiet strength that supports your endeavors without fanfare. When it comes time to raise capital, your reputation for paying bills on time will aid your credibility.

31) *"Good debt is a powerful tool, but bad debt can kill you."*

— Robert Kiyosaki

There is a distinction between good and bad debt. Good debt is used to acquire assets that generate income or appreciation in value, like real estate investments or businesses. Bad debt, on the other hand, involves borrowing for items that depreciate or don't contribute to your financial growth, such as expensive cars or consumer goods. It's like using fire: appropriately harnessed, it can cook your food; uncontrolled, it can burn down your house. Understanding this difference can guide you in making smarter financial decisions that build wealth rather than erode it.

32) "He who will not economize will have to agonize."

— Confucius

Confucius underscores the inevitable consequences of living beyond one's means. Failing to practice frugality leads to financial stress and hardship, agonizing over bills, debts, and unforeseen expenses. It's like ignoring a small leak in a dam; over time, the pressure builds until a catastrophic failure occurs. By adopting a habit of economizing, spending less than you earn, and saving the rest, you build a buffer against life's uncertainties and reduce financial anxiety.

33) "Good times are when people make debts to pay in bad times."

— Robert Quinlin

Robert Quinlin observes the irony that people often incur debts during prosperous periods, leaving them vulnerable during hardships. Leverage is always highest at the top of the bubble.

An illustrative example of Robert Quinlin's observation is the 2008 financial crisis, where during the economic boom of the early 2000s, individuals and financial institutions accumulated excessive debt amid soaring housing prices. Homebuyers took on large mortgages with minimal down payments, often relying on adjustable-rate loans that seemed affordable due to low initial interest rates. Simultaneously, banks and investors heavily leveraged themselves by investing in complex mortgage-backed securities, confident that the good times would last. However, when the housing bubble burst, and interest rates rose, borrowers struggled to meet payments, leading to widespread defaults. The high levels of debt incurred during the prosperous times became unmanageable burdens during the downturn, triggering a cascade of financial failures and a global recession. This scenario vividly demonstrates how debts amassed in good times can become detrimental in bad times, highlighting the dangers of over-leveraging at the peak of economic bubbles and underscoring the importance of prudent financial management.

34) *"Before borrowing money from a friend, decide which you need more."*

— Addison H. Hallock

In the realm of human relationships, money is a volatile force that can corrode even the strongest bonds. To borrow from a friend is to introduce an element of imbalance and unspoken obligation, a tension that few friendships can survive intact. Before you seek immediate financial respite at the expense of personal ties, consider the long-term cost to your mutual trust and goodwill. If you must tread this precarious path, only meticulous clarity and firmly established terms can safeguard the relationship from inevitable decay.

35) *"Debt is the worst poverty."*

— Thomas Fuller

In the intricate web of human struggles, debt stands as a silent tyrant, an unseen poverty more crippling than the lack of material wealth. Thomas Fuller's words unveil a profound truth: debt is a burden that anchors the mind and spirit, an invisible weight that saps our vitality and undermines our autonomy. It is a shackle that binds us not just financially but psychologically, infiltrating our thoughts and eroding our peace. To pursue a life free from debt is to seek a form of liberation that transcends mere monetary gain; it is to attain a richness of the soul and sovereignty over one's destiny. Recognize that true wealth lies not in the accumulation of possessions but in the freedom from the chains that unseen debts forge around our very being.

36) *"The rich rule over the poor, and the borrower is slave to the lender."*

— Proverbs 22:7

In the grand theater of life, the rich stand as the puppet masters while the poor dance to the tune of their whims. Wealth, like a well-forged chain, binds the borrower to the lender, enslaving one to the other's will. This ancient truth reveals a timeless law: those who control resources control the destinies of others.

To avoid becoming a pawn in this relentless game, one must seek to unshackle themselves from debt, for each loan granted is a subtle surrender of autonomy. The path to true power lies in financial independence, where your choices remain your own, free from the grip of another's control.

37) "Debt is the fatal disease of republics, the first thing and the mightiest to undermine governments and corrupt the people."

— Wendell Phillips

Wendell Phillips' observation about debt strikes at the heart of something fundamental: debt, when unchecked, is like a corrosive force, eroding the very structures that uphold society. It's not just a matter of money but of stability and trust. Debt doesn't simply destabilize governments. It creeps into the culture, distorting the values of the people themselves. And that's the real danger: when a society becomes entangled in debt, it loses its capacity to act responsibly and with integrity. Corruption follows, not because individuals suddenly lose their moral compass but because the very incentives and structures around them have been corrupted.

Phillips points to something deeper—a warning that, when taken seriously, calls us to confront the realities of fiscal irresponsibility, not just at the individual level, but collectively. A society that indulges in debt without discipline undermines its future. It loses the trust of its people, the integrity of its institutions, and, ultimately, the capacity to govern itself effectively. The antidote? Responsibility—clear thinking, transparent systems, and a willingness to face the uncomfortable truth that we must maintain balance and order in our economic practices. If we don't, the consequences ripple far beyond economics; they shape the very moral foundation of the society in which we live.

38) *"Some debts are fun when you are acquiring them, but none are fun when you set about retiring them."*

— Ogden Nash

Ogden Nash's quip touches on a profound psychological truth—debt is seductive in the moment of acquisition but merciless in the demands of repayment. It's akin to indulging in short-term pleasure without fully grasping the long-term consequences. The allure of immediate gratification can blind us to the inevitable reality: every debt incurred brings with it a burden, and that burden must be borne eventually.

This speaks to a larger pattern in human behavior. We are wired to seek out what's pleasurable now, often disregarding the future costs. But life is structured in such a way that the future always arrives, and when it does, we face the consequences of our actions. The process of paying off debt—whether financial or metaphorical—is not simply an economic activity but a form of psychological reckoning. It forces us to confront our impulsive nature and acknowledge that, in the end, nothing is truly free.

The solution lies in the ability to delay gratification, to think long-term rather than yielding to the temptation of the immediate. Mindful consumption—knowing not just what we want, but why we want it— can prevent the kind of self-inflicted suffering that comes from indulgence without foresight. The question we must constantly ask ourselves is this: are we trading fleeting enjoyment for future pain? If we can answer that honestly, we stand a better chance of avoiding the traps of debt, both literal and figurative.

39) "If you think nobody cares if you're alive, try missing a couple of car payments."

— Earl Wilson

Earl Wilson cuts straight to the heart of a hidden asymmetry in modern life: you might think you're insignificant but miss a couple of car payments, and you'll quickly discover otherwise. It's a stark reminder of how systems, particularly financial ones, are designed to be unforgiving in their vigilance. The moment you default, the impersonal machinery of debt collection activates with mechanical precision.

This is the nature of the modern financial system: indifferent to your existence until you deviate from the expected path. It's an example of fragility—a small misstep in your financial obligations triggers a disproportionately large response. The system doesn't care about your well-being; it cares about maintaining its own structural integrity, and your failure to pay disrupts that order.

The solution is antifragility in your financial habits. You can't rely on the system's leniency because it doesn't exist. Automate your payments, stay ahead of your obligations, and build redundancies into your life to ensure that you are resilient against the inevitable shocks. In a world of leverage, where you're only as good as your last payment, it's better to structure your life in such a way that you are less exposed to the whims of creditors and the financial apparatus. The key isn't merely staying afloat; it's positioning yourself to benefit from the volatility that will inevitably arise.

40) *"Debt is a tool; wield it wisely, and it can build your future. Use it recklessly, and it will own you."*

— American Saying

Debt is the inevitable shadow cast by the pursuit of wealth. It clings to those who chase fortune without caution, a silent and insidious companion that grows as ambition blinds the seeker. Like a shadow, it appears harmless, unnoticed until the moment it overwhelms. The seduction of wealth lures many into overreaching, confusing the illusion of abundance with real power.

This is the trap: to mistake leverage for success, to believe that accumulating debt is a step toward prosperity when it is a slow erosion of control. True wealth lies not in how much one can acquire but in how much one can retain without becoming accountable to others. To master this game, you must first understand the dangers debt presents, for it is a tool that can either serve you or shackle you.

The wise strategist embraces restraint, knowing real power comes from independence, not the fleeting high of borrowed resources. Protect yourself from the seduction of debt, and you will find that true and unburdened wealth will follow in its own time.

41) "A man in debt is caught in a net."

— French Proverb

Debt is not just a financial obligation; it's a psychological trap. Once you're ensnared, your freedom of movement is restricted. You can no longer act with the autonomy and agency that defines a free individual. It's like being a fish caught in a net, thrashing in vain against the constraints imposed by your past decisions.

Debt is not just a matter of owing money—it's a profound limitation on your potential, future, and capacity to act effectively. Every decision becomes colored by the weight of what you owe, and the longer you stay in that net, the harder it becomes to extricate yourself.

What's the solution? First, it's awareness and understanding that debt is not simply an inconvenience but a genuine barrier to personal growth. Second, it's your responsibility to take active steps to devise a plan, strategize, and move toward freeing yourself from the constraints that bind you. If you can avoid falling into that net in the first place, all the better. But if you're already caught, it's time to confront the hard truth and chart a course toward financial and psychological liberation.

42) *"Debt is a powerful master but a poor servant."*

— Traditional Saying

Debt is a master of ruthless efficiency, wielding control over those who fall under its influence. It commands obedience, dictating terms with unwavering authority, and once you submit to its power, it tightens its grip relentlessly. Like an iron-fisted ruler, debt forces you into a position of vulnerability, where your every action is bound by obligation.

But as a servant, debt is treacherous and unreliable. It may promise you leverage and opportunity, yet it saps your freedom, eroding your capacity to act independently. What seems like a tool for advancement quickly turns into a snare, a weight that grows heavier each day.

To master debt, you must never allow it to master you. Use it sparingly, with caution and precision, understanding that it is a force that can quickly shift from an instrument of power to an unyielding tyrant. The true strategist knows when to wield debt and when to walk away, ensuring that it serves their interests without ever becoming a servant to it.

43) "Debt and lies are usually mixed together."

— François Rabelais

Observes a troubling pattern: debt and lies are often intertwined. Once you're in debt, it's easy to become entangled in deception. Why? Because debt creates pressure, pressure to meet expectations, maintain appearances, and avoid shame. And under that weight, people tend to bend the truth. They hide the extent of their financial struggles, make promises they can't keep, and tell themselves stories to justify their actions.

This is a dangerous path. Lies, like debt, compound over time. A small deception might seem harmless at first, but it snowballs, growing into a web of dishonesty that becomes nearly impossible to untangle. The more you lie, the more you have to lie to cover your tracks and the deeper into the hole you fall.

What's the solution? It's the hard path of truth. Acknowledging your debt to yourself and others is the first step toward solving the problem. Transparency, as uncomfortable as it may be, is crucial. When you're honest about your financial situation, you open the door to real solutions. Deception only makes the situation worse. If you confront reality head-on, no matter how painful, you're far more likely to escape the cycle of debt and lies before it destroys you.

44) "If you have debt, I'm willing to bet that general clutter is a problem for you too."

— Suze Orman

Financial expert Suze Orman parallels financial debt and physical clutter, suggesting both stem from a lack of discipline and organization. Clutter, whether in your home or finances, can create stress and reduce efficiency. It's like trying to find a needle in a haystack. By decluttering your physical space, you may find it easier to organize and manage your finances. Establishing order can lead to better decision-making and a more straightforward path to reducing debt.

Suze Orman's observation points to a broader psychological phenomenon: financial debt and physical clutter often stem from difficulties in self-regulation and cognitive overload. When individuals struggle to manage their environment, whether their spending or their living spaces, it can create an overwhelming sense, leading to disorganization in multiple aspects of life. Clutter, like debt, reflects a buildup of unresolved decisions and postponed responsibilities, which contribute to feelings of stress, anxiety, and a lack of control. The mental clutter from physical disarray can cloud judgment and impair effective decision-making, making it harder to stay disciplined with finances. By addressing one area of disorganization, such as decluttering a living space, individuals may feel more empowered and clear-headed, enabling them to tackle their financial issues with greater focus and resolve.

45) "National debt, if it is not excessive, will be to us a national blessing."

— Alexander Hamilton

Alexander Hamilton, one of the Founding Fathers of the United States, believed that a manageable national debt could be beneficial. It's similar to a business taking out a loan to invest in growth opportunities. A reasonable amount of debt can help build creditworthiness and fund essential projects. However, the key is moderation and prudent management. This principle can be applied personally by ensuring any debt taken on is sustainable and contributes positively to your financial well-being.

Alexander Hamilton's perspective on the national debt as a potential blessing can be illustrated by how businesses or individuals use debt to generate growth. Imagine a small business owner who takes out a loan to invest in new equipment or expand operations. If the debt is manageable and strategically used, it can lead to higher revenues, improved productivity, and, ultimately, more wealth. In this way, the debt becomes a tool for growth rather than a burden.

On a national scale, when a country borrows responsibly, it can invest in infrastructure, education, or technological advancements, which stimulate economic growth, create jobs, and improve the overall standard of living. As Hamilton suggested, the key is ensuring that the debt remains sustainable so the benefits outweigh the costs, just like with personal debt. The danger comes when debt becomes excessive, leading to instability, but when used wisely, it can open doors to long-term prosperity.

46) *"Getting into debt is getting into a tanglesome net."*

— Zora Neale Hurston

Debt isn't just a financial burden; it's a trap that ensnares you in ways you might not fully realize until you're caught. At first, taking on debt can seem harmless, even beneficial. It feels like you're moving forward. But the deeper you get, the more restricted your movement becomes, and suddenly, you're entangled in obligations that dictate your future actions.

It's a classic example of how short-term thinking can lead to long-term suffering. People often walk into debt without considering the full ramifications, focusing on immediate gains while ignoring the constraints they impose on their future selves. Hurston's warning is clear: before you step into that net, ask yourself if you can extricate yourself when the time comes. Debt may solve a problem today, but it can easily create more problems tomorrow, limiting your freedom and constraining your potential. The challenge is thinking ahead, acting cautiously, and avoiding traps that compromise your autonomy.

47) *"Debt is like a person who does not sleep or tire, but constantly pursues its prey."*

— African Proverb

Debt is the most relentless of adversaries, an unyielding force that neither sleeps nor tires. It stalks its prey with quiet persistence, constantly advancing, never retreating. Like a shadow that clings to you in light and darkness, debt follows with a singular aim: to tighten its grip and drain you of your autonomy.

The wisdom of this African proverb lies in its recognition of debt's insidious nature. It is not merely an inconvenience; it is a predator, patient and unforgiving. Those who fail to grasp this truth will be caught in an endless pursuit, running from a foe that never rests.

To defeat such a pursuer, one must be vigilant and strategic. You cannot ignore debt, hoping it will disappear. Instead, confront it with deliberate action—a clear plan to sever its hold before it tightens beyond escape. The true master knows the only way to outpace debt is to act swiftly, cutting it down before it consumes you entirely.

48) "There's nothing wrong with looking into the future, but don't borrow trouble."

— Traditional Proverb

The wisdom of this traditional proverb is simple but profound: planning ahead is essential, but acting recklessly in anticipation of future events invites unnecessary risk. Borrowing trouble is like leveraging yourself to the hilt before the storm arrives. You're amplifying your exposure to downside risks without knowing if the bridge will collapse under the weight.

This is the essence of fragility. By taking on unnecessary burdens or debt, you make your system more vulnerable to random shocks and black swan events. Instead, prepare for volatility by making decisions that are robust under uncertainty. Minimize your downside while maintaining optionality. Don't amplify potential failure; instead, set yourself up to benefit from the unexpected.

49) *"Think what you do when you run into debt; you give another power over your liberty. "*

— Benjamin Franklin

There is a loss of personal freedom that comes with indebtedness. Owing money can limit your choices and obligate you to others' terms, much like signing away certain rights. It's comparable to handing over the keys to your life. Being mindful of this potential loss of autonomy can encourage more careful financial decisions, prioritizing saving and spending within your means.

50) "If you are going to use debt, make sure it's productive debt used to acquire appreciating assets."

— Grant Cardone

Grant Cardone, a real estate mogul and author, emphasizes using debt strategically to build wealth. Productive debt is borrowed money invested in assets that increase in value or generate income, such as real estate or a business. It's like planting seeds in fertile ground. You expect growth over time. Conversely, using debt to purchase depreciating assets, like cars or consumer goods, can hinder your financial progress. For example, using debt to buy real estate, stocks, or businesses can be a wise move in certain circumstances, while debt for consumer goods can cripple your future. Understanding the difference ensures that if you take on debt, it works for you, not against you.

51) "Never make an interest-free loan. Either gift the money, or structure a proper deal"

— Angelo Hunter

Interest-free loans may seem like a kind gesture, but they often lead to unintended consequences. When you lend money without interest, you remove the natural incentive for the borrower to prioritize repayment. Without a cost attached to the loan, there is no urgency or pressure to return the funds, leading to complacency or neglect. There is always something better that the borrower can do with their money, even just leaving it in a lower interesting savings account. This will strain relationships, as the borrower may come to see the loan as a favor with no real obligation. In this way, interest-free loans often create a dynamic where the lender feels taken advantage of while the borrower lacks the necessary motivation or incentive to repay promptly.

The alternative is far cleaner: either gift the money or structure a proper deal. A gift carries no expectations and frees both parties from future complications, allowing goodwill to remain intact. Structuring a formal agreement with clear terms ensures accountability and mutual respect, as the borrower understands the value of the loan and the responsibility to repay it. By charging interest or setting terms, you create an incentive for timely repayment and preserve the integrity of the relationship, avoiding the pitfalls of ambiguity or resentment. In money matters, clarity and intention are key to maintaining trust and balance.

52) *"Interest on debts grows without rain."*

— Yiddish Proverb

Debt is like a creeping shadow, stretching longer and darker the more you try to ignore it. Unlike the crops in the field, it doesn't need a drop of water to thrive. It grows silently in the dead of night, under a clear sky or a stormy one, indifferent to your situation. That's the sinister truth behind this proverb: interest doesn't wait. It piles up, day after day, whether you're ready for it or not, like some lurking horror in the attic, getting fatter while you sleep.

Ignore it too long, and what seemed like a minor inconvenience turns into a full-blown monster, gnawing at your peace of mind. It's not just the numbers going up; it's the weight pressing down on your chest and the dread curling around you. The only way out? You have to act fast. Pay more than the bare minimum, chop down the high-interest debts first, and for God's sake, don't dig the hole deeper by borrowing more. It's not a matter of just saving money. It's about escaping something that, left unchecked, will swallow you whole.

53) *"Debt is dumb. Cash is king."*

— Dave Ramsey

In the theater of personal and financial power, Dave Ramsey's proclamation serves as a strategic maxim for those who seek mastery over their destinies. Debt is an invisible shackle, binding individuals to obligations that erode autonomy and foster dependency. It diminishes one's ability to act independently, forcing priorities to align with creditors rather than personal aspirations. History is replete with the rise and fall of empires and individuals alike, undone by the seductive allure of leverage, only to be crushed under the weight of their ambitions.

Conversely, cash embodies the ultimate form of capital: liquid, sovereign, and empowering. It grants immediate authority, enabling decisive action and seizing opportunities without the encumbrance of financial obligations. Possessing cash is akin to holding the keys to one's fortress, allowing for strategic maneuvering and resilience against unforeseen adversities. In the grand chessboard of life, those prioritizing cash over debt position themselves as masters of their fate, navigating complexities with clarity and strength and achieving enduring power and unassailable independence.

54) "A debt may get moldy, but it never decays."

— Philip Stanhope, 4th Earl of Chesterfield

Debt is like a ticking time bomb, hidden in the corner of your life, slowly counting down while you go about your day. You might not see or hear it at first, but it's always lurking, waiting for the right moment to explode. Ignore it too long, and what starts as something small. a late bill here, a forgotten loan there. Becomes a much bigger problem. Interest piles up, penalties kick in, and before you know it, the whole thing's out of control.

The key is to act before it's too late. You don't wait around for a problem like that to solve itself. You get ahead of it. Check your debts, make a plan, and deal with them one by one, like taking down enemies in a fight. You can't afford to let them fester. Because once they blow up, they'll take everything down with them. Keep your eyes open, stay sharp, and never let a debt catch you off guard.

55) "When you get in debt, you become a slave."

— Andrew Jackson

Ah, debt, the invisible chain by which the weak willingly bind themselves. To be in debt is to surrender your will to another, to place your life in the hands of forces beyond your control. How insidious, this quiet slavery! It does not demand submission openly but works subtly, gnawing at your autonomy and dictating your choices under the guise of necessity. Debt is not merely a burden; it is a self-imposed mastery, where the debtor cowers beneath the weight of what he owes, his every action shadowed by the creditor's looming presence.

Jackson's warning is a call to resist this modern form of servitude. But what is financial independence if not a triumph of the will? To live within one's means is not mere prudence; it is the assertion of power over one's destiny. It is the refusal to bow to the external chains that society so easily wraps around its unsuspecting followers. Only the free man, free from debt and obligation, can walk with dignity in this world. The rest, those enslaved by their desires, must serve masters they cannot see, forever shackled to the consequences of their weakness.

56) "The only man who sticks closer to you in adversity than a friend is a creditor."

— Unknown Author

In moments of hardship, when friends may waver, and support fades, one figure will always remain by your side: the creditor. Unlike friends, whose loyalty can be swayed by circumstance, the creditor is bound not by emotion but by cold obligation. Their presence is relentless, clinging to you with a tenacity that far exceeds the loyalty of any companion. They are there not out of concern for your well-being but to enforce the contract you've entered, holding your feet to the fire when the world around you collapses.

This truth reveals the harsh reality of debt. It doesn't pause for your struggles nor sympathize with your plight. It sharpens the edges of your adversity, adding another layer of stress to an already fragile situation. The creditor's persistence, while predictable, is a reminder that debt, if not managed with precision, can become an adversary in itself. The wise maneuver is to prepare in times of fortune, building reserves and confronting debt before it tightens its grip. Open dialogue and proactive strategy can mitigate its sting, but make no mistake, the creditor, unlike a friend, is always waiting, and he does not forget.

57) *"Debts are like children: the smaller they are, the more noise they make."*

— Spanish Proverb

This proverb offers a striking comparison between small debts and children and speaks to a fundamental truth about responsibility. As a crying infant demands your immediate attention, so do small debts clamor for resolution. They're not insignificant because they're small. It's precisely because they are manageable that they nag at you, like a reminder of what you're neglecting. It's an echo of chaos, a sign that something minor needs to be set right before it spirals out of control.

In life, it's often the small things that, if left unchecked, can grow into overwhelming burdens. A tiny debt might seem harmless at first, easily brushed aside. But over time, it accumulates, and the noise gets louder, compounding interest and mounting stress until it becomes a real problem. The lesson here is clear: confront the small things, the minor responsibilities, while they are still manageable. Take control of them before they take control of you. It's not just about maintaining financial order; it's about establishing discipline and sovereignty over your life, reducing unnecessary chaos in the future.

58) "It defies logic that protections against predatory debt collection practices don't apply to debt collectors hired by the federal government."

— Cory Booker

Cory Booker exposes a structural flaw in the system that seems almost too obvious to overlook. The very protections designed to shield citizens from aggressive debt collection are arbitrarily absent when the creditor is the government. It's an apparent contradiction. Rules that apply in the private sector are inexplicably suspended when the state itself is involved. In a world where power dynamics are skewed, this gap isn't just a policy oversight; it's a feature of a system that doesn't want to protect everyone equally.

From a strategic perspective, it reveals a broader issue: systems are often designed to perpetuate themselves, and reform requires not just an adjustment of policies but a shift in the underlying assumptions. If you want real change, you can't just patch the holes in the net, and you have to question why the holes were there in the first place. In the meantime, your defense lies in knowledge. Understanding where the system falls short empowers you to navigate it precisely, leveraging whatever protections are available.

59) *"It is not only our duty but our moral obligation to break from the oppression of debt. We must rise above the political considerations and do what is right for the future of our nation."*

— Dan Coats

Debt is not just a financial issue. It's a moral one. It weighs heavily on individuals, families, and entire societies, eroding the foundation upon which stability and progress are built. In a sense, debt represents a kind of bondage, a self-imposed limitation that stifles growth and opportunity. It's not merely an economic problem to be solved through policy tinkering or political maneuvering; it's a more profound, ethical responsibility. We owe ourselves, our communities, and future generations to rise above the burden of overindebtedness.

Every financial decision you make reverberates beyond the immediate moment. Your debt isn't just a private concern; it impacts your ability to contribute meaningfully to society. If you are shackled by debt, your potential is constrained. The moral obligation, then, is to manage your finances with discipline and foresight. Doing so frees yourself and sets a standard for others to follow. You become an agent of positive change, showing that the path forward is one of responsibility, not indulgence, and that true freedom begins with breaking the chains of debt, both personally and collectively.

60) "Leverage is the key to building wealth in real estate."

— Robert G. Allen

Leverage, in its most powerful form, is not just about amplifying returns. It's about unlocking asymmetric outcomes. In real estate, you gain control of valuable assets with minimal upfront capital, turning borrowed money into an engine of wealth creation. This is the fundamental concept: small inputs with outsized returns. It's how you bend reality in your favor, achieving what would be impossible with limited resources. The more leverage you use wisely, the faster you can scale.

However, leverage is a double-edged sword. In the same way it accelerates gains, it can magnify losses, especially in volatile markets. The key is not just in using leverage but in understanding the broader context, property cycles, market dynamics, and debt management. Most investors think linearly, but those who master leverage think exponentially. It's not just about lifting a heavy weight with a small effort. It's about controlling that weight and knowing when to put it down before it crushes you. Success hinges on informed, calculated risks, taking positions where the downside is minimized but the upside remains exponential.

61) "Debt is a mistake between lender and borrower."

— John R. Smith

Debt often arises from poor decisions on both sides. Imagine two dancers out of sync; both are responsible for the misstep. The lender may have been careless in extending credit, while the borrower might have overestimated their ability to repay. It highlights the importance of due diligence and honesty in financial dealings, echoing the age-old wisdom that "it takes two to tango." Before entering into a lending or borrowing agreement, both parties should assess the terms and ensure they are mutually beneficial and sustainable.

62) "I'm the king of debt. I love debt."

— Donald Trump

Throughout his career, Trump has strategically used debt to finance large real estate projects. By borrowing money, he's been able to take on big ventures without relying entirely on his own funds. This approach allows him to increase his investment power, purchase high-value properties, and grow his portfolio quickly. Using borrowed capital can boost potential returns and show confidence in managing and repaying debt responsibly. Additionally, embracing debt can demonstrate financial strength and a proactive growth mindset, making him a strong competitor in the real estate markets as a younger man.

63) "When credit is expanded beyond the natural level, it leads to malinvestments that eventually must be liquidated in a recession."

— Ludwig von Mises

Imagine the economy as a grand party, and credit is the lifeblood that keeps the festivities buzzing. Ludwig von Mises warns that when we crank up the credit beyond its natural flow, it's like serving endless appetizers without checking if everyone can handle more. Initially, everything seems exciting and prosperous: businesses expand, investments soar, and optimism reigns. However, this overindulgence in borrowing leads to "malinvestments," or poor financial decisions fueled by easy money. Just as an overfilled party eventually spills out of control, these misguided investments become unsustainable. When reality catches up, a recession hits, forcing everyone to clean up the mess by liquidating those shaky ventures. Mises' insight serves as a valuable reminder that balance in credit is crucial to maintaining a healthy, thriving economy, preventing the inevitable downturn that follows excessive borrowing.

64) "Borrowing is for suckers."

— Charlie Munger

Charlie Munger, the legendary investor and vice chairman of Berkshire Hathaway, famously declared, "Borrowing is for suckers." At first glance, this blunt statement might seem dismissive of the strategic use of debt in business and personal finance. He advocates for financial prudence and emphasizes the power of owning assets outright rather than relying on borrowed money. By avoiding debt, individuals and businesses can maintain greater control over their finances, reduce risk, and build wealth more sustainably.

65) "You cannot spend your way out of recession or borrow your way out of debt."

— Daniel Hannan

Excessive spending and borrowing aren't solutions to financial problems. It's like attempting to extinguish a fire with gasoline, the very act exacerbates the issue. On a personal scale, using credit to pay off credit leads to a cycle of increasing debt. Instead, addressing the root causes, reducing expenses, increasing income, and creating a realistic budget, can pave the way out of financial hardship. Hannan's message encourages us to confront challenges directly rather than seeking quick fixes that may worsen the situation.

66) *"Leverage is a source of fragility; it amplifies both gains and losses, making systems more vulnerable to unexpected shocks."*

— Nassim Taleb

Leverage, as Nassim Taleb articulates, is inherently a source of fragility because it doesn't just magnify potential gains but equally amplifies losses, thereby exposing systems to heightened vulnerability when unexpected shocks occur. Imagine leverage as a lever that can boost your returns when everything goes smoothly, enticing investors and institutions with the promise of higher profits. However, this same leverage can turn disastrous with even minor adverse events, as the amplified losses can cascade into catastrophic failures, much like what transpired during the 2008 financial crisis. Taleb underscores that leveraged systems operate on precarious margins of safety, thriving only in stable, predictable environments. In the face of Black Swan events— rare and unforeseen disruptions—leverage transforms from a tool for growth into a mechanism for collapse. Thus, while leverage offers the allure of enhanced returns, it simultaneously embeds significant hidden vulnerabilities, making resilience and antifragility far more crucial for enduring the unpredictable nature of the real world.

67) *"A public debt is a public curse."*

— James Madison

Madison strikes at the heart of a nation's long-term stability. While often seen as an abstract issue, the national debt is like a silent thief, gradually robbing society of its future prosperity. When a country borrows excessively, the weight of that debt eventually falls on the shoulders of its citizens, often through higher taxes, reduced social services, and limited public investment in critical areas like education and infrastructure. It creates a cycle where the fiscal irresponsibility of the present burdens future generations. We must take collective responsibility for budgetary matters, recognizing that a nation's financial health is everyone's concern. Just as personal debt can strain an individual's well-being, public debt can erode a society's potential, making it crucial for individuals and governments to manage resources prudently to ensure a stable, thriving future.

68) *"Be wary when you use debt, it is an obligation to your future self that you will not want"*

— Angelo Hunter

Debt, while often seen as a tool for growth, carries a hidden cost beyond interest rates and repayment terms. When you borrow, you are committing on behalf of your future self, binding them to today's decisions. What feels like a reasonable trade-off in the present can quickly become a burden that limits your options and freedom down the line. Over time, this financial obligation can grow heavy, consuming your energy, resources, and mental space as it follows you into the future. In this way, debt locks you into a cycle that may constrain your ability to take advantage of new opportunities or respond to unforeseen challenges.

The danger of debt lies not just in the monetary repayment but in the emotional and psychological toll it takes over time. As circumstances change, what once seemed like a manageable commitment can become a source of regret or resentment toward your past decisions. You may find that the obligations you willingly took on now stand in the way of your aspirations, forcing your future self to prioritize debt over more fulfilling or profitable endeavors. This subtle erosion of freedom makes debt a hazardous tool when used carelessly. Approach it cautiously, always mindful of the weight it places on the future you may not yet fully understand.

69) "I've borrowed knowing that you can pay back with discounts. And I've done very well."

— Donald Trump

Donald Trump used debt as part of his strategic approach to business. He emphasizes borrowing money to negotiate later to repay it for less than the total amount through discounts, restructuring, or settlements. By doing so, he effectively reduces his financial obligations, allowing him to profit from using leverage. Trump credits this approach for much of his economic success, as he gained an advantage by borrowing and minimizing the repayment cost. This tactic is expected in the business world, particularly in industries like real estate, where debt management is crucial to profitability.

70) "One of the greatest disservices you can do a man is to lend him money that he can't pay back."

— Jesse H. Jones

There is a fundamental flaw in careless lending: it's a short-term fix with long-term consequences. Lending irresponsibly is like handing someone a tool they're not equipped to use. Sure, they get what they need at the moment, but without the right safeguards, it's bound to fail. Before you offer capital, ask whether the borrower is positioned for success. Thoughtful lending isn't just about giving money; it's about ensuring the person can generate enough value to repay it without collapsing under pressure. Consider modern student loan lending practices for a modern example of distorted lending practices.

71) "In the midst of life, we are in debt."

— Ethel Watts Mumford

Mumford captures the quiet but constant presence of debt in our daily existence. It's like a shadow that follows us, often unnoticed but always there, subtly influencing our decisions and shaping our financial landscape. Mumford's reflection urges us to recognize the pervasive nature of debt and how it impacts our lives, even when it seems invisible. The key is to remain vigilant, regularly managing and reassessing our financial obligations to ensure that debt doesn't grow unchecked or become a burden too heavy to bear.

72) "I understand debt better than probably anybody. I know how to deal with debt. I love debt."

— Donald Trump

Donald Trump has long embraced debt as a strategic tool in his business ventures, using it to fund major real estate acquisitions and navigate financial challenges. One of his most notable examples is his handling of the Trump Taj Mahal casino, where he leveraged bankruptcy to restructure over $3 billion in debt, reducing his personal liability while maintaining control of the asset. Throughout the 1990s, his casinos in Atlantic City faced multiple bankruptcies, but Trump consistently renegotiated terms with creditors to minimize his financial losses. He used debt to his advantage, seeing it as a way to amplify gains when successful and shield himself from risk when projects faltered, showcasing his ability to manage and manipulate debt as a business tactic.

73) "Artificially low interest rates distort the structure of production by encouraging investments that are not supported by consumer savings."

— Ludwig von Mises

When interest rates are kept low, businesses and investors are incentivized to borrow and invest in projects that may seem profitable because the cost of borrowing is cheap. However, these investments aren't always supported by actual consumer demand or sufficient savings. In essence, the low rates falsely signal that more resources are available than there are, leading to a misallocation of capital. This can result in a boom period with overinvestment in projects that eventually become unsustainable, leading to economic downturns or crashes when the market corrects itself. Mises reminds us that tampering with interest rates can disrupt the natural balance between savings and investment, causing instability in the long run.

74) "Credit is a system whereby a person who can't pay gets another person who can't pay to guarantee that he can pay."

— Charles Dickens

Charles Dickens satirically criticizes the flawed nature of some credit systems. It's like a row of dominoes where each piece relies on the next to stay upright; if one falls, they all do. The quote highlights the importance of sound financial practices and skepticism of systems built on shaky foundations. Understanding the risks involved in co-signing or guaranteeing loans can prevent potential financial disasters.

75) "Debt can be a tool if it helps you achieve your financial goals."

— Suze Orman

When used strategically, debt can be a powerful tool for achieving financial goals. Borrowing money can help you reach significant milestones, such as buying a home, pursuing higher education, or starting a business. Just like a hammer helps build something valuable when used properly, debt can create opportunities for growth and long-term stability. The key is managing it wisely, only taking on debt that is affordable, aligned with your goals, and offers a clear return on investment. Before borrowing, it's essential to weigh the long-term benefits against the costs, ensuring that the debt will contribute positively to your financial future rather than becoming a burden.

76) *"Live like no one else, so later you can live like no one else."*

— Dave Ramsey

Dave Ramsey's quote emphasizes the importance of making sacrifices and practicing financial discipline early in life to achieve long-term financial freedom. The first part, "Live like no one else," suggests adopting a lifestyle of frugality, budgeting, and avoiding unnecessary debt, even if it means living differently from others who may prioritize short-term pleasures. By doing this, the second part, "so later you can live like no one else," becomes possible, where you can enjoy the rewards of financial independence and security, free from debt, allowing you to live a more abundant and stress-free life than most. It's a call to make short-term sacrifices for long-term gain.

77) "A mortgage casts a shadow on the sunniest field."

— Robert G. Ingersoll

Debt, even in the best of circumstances, can dim our enjoyment of life's brightest moments. It's like seeing a beautiful, sunlit landscape but feeling the weight of a looming cloud. Ingersoll's point is clear: while opportunities may arise, financial obligations, especially long-term ones like a mortgage, can temper our ability to seize or fully enjoy them. The message here is to be cautious about the debts we take on, as they can quietly overshadow our freedom and peace of mind, even when everything else is going well. Understanding this allows us to navigate life more mindfully, balancing ambition with financial clarity.

78) *"Debt is the secret foe of thrift, as vice and idleness are its open foes."*

— James H. Aughey

Debt is the silent enemy of thrift, just as vice and laziness are its more obvious foes. James H. Aughey reminds us that while some threats to our finances are easy to spot, debt quietly erodes our efforts to save, much like unseen cracks in a foundation. Recognizing debt as a hidden danger can strengthen our resolve to live within our means and build a more secure financial future.

79) "It is the debtor that is ruined by hard times."

— Rutherford B. Hayes

Those burdened with debt are the most vulnerable when economic storms hit. It's like a tree with shallow roots. What seems sturdy in fair weather is quickly uprooted in a storm. In difficult times, debt can become an unbearable weight, amplifying financial stress and leaving little room for recovery. Hayes' message is a call to strengthen our financial foundations by minimizing debt, building emergency funds, and planning wisely. By doing so, we protect ourselves from ruin and build resilience, enabling us to weather tough times with greater security and confidence.

80) *"The expansion of credit is always accompanied by an unsustainable boom, which ultimately results in a bust."*

— Ludwig von Mises

Ludwig von Mises' quote suggests that when credit is artificially expanded, typically through easy lending and low interest rates, it fuels an unsustainable economic boom. During this period, businesses and individuals borrow more, creating the illusion of strong growth. However, this boom is not based on genuine increases in productivity or value but rather on inflated access to credit. Eventually, the limitations of this over-extension become apparent, leading to a collapse—known as a bust—where businesses fail, debts cannot be repaid, and the economy contracts. Mises warns that while credit expansion may temporarily boost the economy, it inevitably results in an economic downturn.

81) "There are no shortcuts when it comes to getting out of debt."

— Dave Ramsey

Eliminating debt requires hard work and discipline. It's like climbing a mountain; there's no elevator to the top. The process may be challenging, but it's also rewarding, teaching valuable lessons about perseverance and financial responsibility along the way. Developing a realistic plan and sticking to it is essential for success.

82) "I've made a fortune by using debt, and if things don't work out, I renegotiate the debt. That's a smart thing, not a stupid thing."

— Donald Trump

Donald Trump's quote offers an intriguing look into how he uses debt as a financial tool, turning what many see as a burden into an opportunity. He's saying that borrowing money isn't something to fear—if done wisely, it can help you take on bigger projects and create wealth. But here's the twist: if a deal goes sideways, he doesn't panic. Instead, he renegotiates the terms, finding a way to make it work in his favor. It's like playing chess with debt, always thinking a few moves ahead. The lesson here? Debt, when used strategically, can be a powerful ally, and knowing when to pivot and adjust is what separates smart money management from risky behavior. It's not just about borrowing—it's about staying flexible and always being one step ahead.

83) "The borrower runs in his own debt."

— Ralph Waldo Emerson

Emerson implies that borrowers entangle themselves in their obligations. It's akin to weaving a web that ultimately traps oneself. By choosing to borrow, we may inadvertently create obstacles for our future selves. This emphasizes the importance of thoughtful decision-making regarding taking on debt and considering long-term implications.

84) "The debt we owe to the play of imagination is incalculable."

— Carl Jung

Carl Jung shifts the focus to a positive form of debt—our indebtedness to creativity and imagination. It's like a wellspring that nourishes innovation and progress. Acknowledging this "debt" inspires us to value and cultivate our imaginative capacities, enriching our lives and societies. Investing time in creative pursuits can lead to personal fulfillment and breakthroughs in various fields.

85) "Let us all be happy and live within our means, even if we have to borrow the money to do it with."

— Charles Farrar Browne

Browne humorously exposes the irony of borrowing to maintain a lifestyle we can't afford. It's like using a bucket with holes to bail water out of a sinking ship, an unsustainable and counterproductive solution. Browne's satire reminds us that true happiness doesn't come from accumulating debt to keep up appearances; it comes from finding a balance between our desires and our resources. The real key to lasting contentment lies in financial discipline and understanding that living within our means is not a burden but a freedom that protects us from the stress and instability of debt.

86) "Using leverage is an art. If you can use it wisely, it can make you very rich."

— Donald Trump

Leverage, in its essence, is a tool, one that allows you to amplify your resources beyond their natural limits. But like any form of power, it must be handled with precision and foresight. Imagine it as a sharp blade; in skilled hands, it can easily cut through obstacles, allowing you to ascend rapidly. Yet, if wielded carelessly, it can turn against you, leading to ruin. To master leverage is to understand its dual nature: an ally to the disciplined and a peril to the reckless. The art lies in knowing when to push, when to retreat, and always maintaining control. In the game of wealth and power, leverage is your servant, not your master.

87) "Debt-driven economic growth is inherently unstable and prone to crises when the repayment of debts becomes untenable."

— Ludwig von Mises

There are risks that come with fueling progress on borrowed money. While debt can stimulate short-term growth and create the illusion of prosperity, it's a fragile foundation. When the time comes to repay those debts and the economy falters, the consequences can be severe: think financial crises, collapses in confidence, and spiraling interest burdens. This instability highlights the importance of sustainable growth rooted in productivity and innovation rather than excessive reliance on borrowing. For both individuals and nations, this principle underscores the need for careful financial management, as over-leveraging today can lead to economic turmoil tomorrow. Understanding this dynamic can help readers make more prudent financial decisions, both personally and in business.

88) "The national debt is not a side issue; it is the single biggest cause of national weakness."

— Pat Buchanan

The national debt isn't some distant, abstract problem, it's the silent rot in the country's bones. Imagine a towering fortress, strong and imposing on the outside, but its foundations are crumbling within. Brick by brick, the weight of debt weakens everything, and one day, the walls will come tumbling down. No matter how grand or powerful a nation appears, excessive debt gnaws away at its core, making it vulnerable and fragile. This isn't just an issue for economists and politicians; it's a ticking time bomb that could collapse a society from the inside. Buchanan's warning is clear: without fiscal responsibility, even the mightiest fortress can fall.

89) "Interest works night and day in fair weather and foul. It gnaws at a man's substance with invisible teeth. "

— Henry Ward Beecher

Henry Ward Beecher's words give interest a life of its own, like some ravenous creature lurking just out of sight. It doesn't sleep. It doesn't care if the sun is shining or if a storm is howling outside. It just keeps eating away at everything you've worked for, gnawing with invisible teeth, relentless, like termites burrowing through the foundation of your life. You don't notice it at first, but the damage is done by the time you do. That's the nature of interest, and it's a quiet horror. The only way to stop it? Pay down your debt before it chews through everything before it leaves nothing but space where your security used to be.

90) "Act your wage."

— Dave Ramsey

You don't need to chase after a lifestyle you can't afford. Instead, think of it as aligning your spending with what you actually earn. Just because something is tempting or flashy doesn't mean it's worth the financial stress. Ramsey's advice pushes us to prioritize smart budgeting, financial discipline, and long-term goals over short-term gratification. By acting your wage today, you build the foundation for economic freedom and future opportunities.

91) "Sound money is essential to prevent the excessive accumulation of debt and to maintain economic stability."

— Ludwig von Mises

Ludwig von Mises' quote emphasizes the critical role of "sound money" in keeping an economy stable and debt under control. But what exactly does that mean? Sound money is a currency that holds its value over time without being manipulated or inflated recklessly. When money is stable, people and businesses can make smarter financial decisions, and there's less temptation to pile on debt they can't handle. Without it, the economy can spiral into chaos. Think of it like a sturdy foundation. If it crumbles, everything built on top is at risk. Mises essentially says that sound money is the unsung hero of financial health, preventing the economy from collapsing under excessive debt. A stable currency isn't just nice to have. It's the glue that holds everything together. Consider who's fiscal policy will defend the country's currency when voting.

92) "In prosperity, prepare for a change; in adversity, hope for one."

— James Burgh

When things are going great, don't get too comfortable; never lose hope when life gets tough. It's like a captain who tightens the ship's ropes when the weather's perfect, knowing the storm could hit any time, but stays optimistic when the waves are crashing, confident the skies will clear. When your financial seas are smooth, use that time to prepare, save up, reduce debt, and plan for the future. And when adversity strikes, don't panic. Keep your head up because even the roughest storms eventually pass, and the tide always turns.

93) "Debt is like a cancer that slowly eats away at your freedom."

— Michael Mihalik

Michael Mihalik's comparison of debt to cancer hits hard because it's true: debt slowly chips away at your freedom, often without you even noticing at first. Just like cancer can quietly spread before the symptoms show, debt sneaks up and starts limiting your choices, your opportunities, and your peace of mind. Don't wait until debt takes control of your life. Recognize its power early, tackle it head-on, and reclaim your financial freedom before it quietly robs you of your future options. Debt might be sneaky, but with the right approach, you can beat it before it beats you.

94) "The way to become rich is to put all your eggs in one basket and then watch that basket."

— Andrew Carnegie

There is a power of focused effort and attention in wealth-building. While the strategy may appear risky, Carnegie emphasizes that success comes from placing your resources where you have the most confidence and then carefully tending to that investment, much like nurturing a single crop for a successful harvest. In financial terms, this suggests not spreading yourself too thin but concentrating on a well-researched investment or venture, managing it diligently, and avoiding reckless debt. This disciplined approach can yield greater rewards by allowing you to harness the full potential of your efforts.

95) *"Debt is like a drug; it feels good when you take it, but there are consequences to the addiction."*

— Financial Wisdom Saying

This saying likens debt to substance abuse, providing temporary relief but leading to long-term harm. The quote captures the seductive yet destructive nature of borrowing. Like a quick fix, taking on debt can offer short-term satisfaction, masking immediate financial pressures, but over time, the addiction to credit leads to mounting interest, stress, and loss of financial control. The allure is tempting, but the long-term consequences are often devastating, eroding freedom and security. This analogy serves as a warning to approach debt cautiously, emphasizing the importance of financial discipline to avoid being trapped in a cycle of dependence.

96) "Achieving financial freedom is more about how you manage and allocate your resources than how much you earn."

— Naval Ravikant

Wealth isn't just a result of high income but of smart financial habits. Financial independence stems from careful planning, disciplined saving, and strategic investing rather than simply chasing a bigger paycheck. No matter your earnings, the true path to financial freedom lies in making your money work for you, prioritizing long-term stability over short-term gratification. This mindset shift can transform how we view our finances, putting the focus on sustainability, control, and peace of mind.

97) "He that goes a borrowing, goes a sorrowing."

— Thomas Tusser

Just as a moth is irresistibly drawn to a flame, the allure of borrowing can offer immediate relief or satisfaction, ultimately leading to lasting regret and financial strain. This wisdom encourages us to approach credit with caution, highlighting the importance of financial discipline and the peace that comes from living within our means. By understanding and internalizing this message, readers can make more informed decisions, avoiding the pitfalls of indebtedness and fostering a sense of security and well-being in their lives.

98) "When you combine ignorance and leverage, you get some pretty interesting results."

— Warren Buffett

Imagine trying to juggle flaming torches while riding a unicycle. Without the right skills, the outcome is nothing short of disastrous. Buffett warns that using borrowed money or amplified financial tools without a solid understanding is a recipe for chaos. Leverage can magnify your gains, but without the knowledge to manage them, they can quickly become overwhelming losses. This quote is a thrilling reminder that financial literacy is your safety net, transforming leverage from a risky tightrope walk into a strategic dance. By educating yourself and approaching debt with caution, you can harness the power of leverage to build wealth instead of letting ignorance lead you into financial freefall.

99) "Financing debt by printing money can lead to inflation, eroding the value of savings and destabilizing the economy."

— Thomas Sowell

Thomas Sowell's quote is a clear warning about the dangers of trying to finance debt by simply printing more money. It might sound like an easy fix—just make more cash! But here's the catch: flooding the economy with extra money can spark inflation, where prices rise, and the value of your savings slowly melts away like ice cream on a hot day. Over time, this can destabilize the entire economy, making everyday items more expensive while your money buys less and less. The lesson here? There's no magic fix for debt, and printing money isn't a free pass—it's a risky move that could cause more harm than good in the long run. Real financial stability comes from smarter solutions, not shortcuts.

100) "Never loan your car to anyone to whom you have given birth."

— Erma Bombeck

Erma Bombeck's witty advice is a playful way of saying: "Your kids might not treat your stuff with the same care you do!" It's a funny but relatable reminder that lending anything valuable, even to family, can come with risks. Whether it's a car, a favorite sweater, or something sentimental, handing it over might mean seeing it return in less-than-perfect condition. The takeaway? Love your kids, but set clear expectations when sharing your prized possessions to protect both your relationships and your stuff. It's all about finding that balance between generosity and caution!

101) "Financial leverage can accelerate wealth creation when used judiciously."

— Peter Lynch

Peter Lynch, a renowned investor, acknowledges that leverage can boost wealth if applied wisely. It's like adding a sail to a boat; it can increase speed but requires skillful handling to navigate safely. Understanding the mechanics and risks of leverage is essential to harness its benefits without incurring significant losses.

102) "Debt is a powerful tool to magnify gains in investing."

— Warren Buffett

Warren Buffett notes that debt, when used strategically, can enhance investment returns. It's like using a magnifying glass to intensify sunlight; it can create fire but must be handled carefully. Buffett advises caution, emphasizing that only those who thoroughly understand the risks should employ leverage in investments.

103) "Debt, when used wisely, can be a catalyst for growth."

— Mark Cuban

Mark Cuban highlights that strategic borrowing can fuel business expansion and opportunities. It's akin to adding fuel to a rocket—properly managed, it propels you forward. However, misuse can lead to explosive outcomes. Evaluating the potential return on investment and ensuring you can manage repayments are critical when using debt for growth.

104) *"Leverage allows you to control more assets than you could otherwise, increasing your potential returns."*

— Benjamin Graham

Benjamin Graham, known as the father of value investing, points out that leverage enables investors to amplify their market positions. It's like using a telescope to see farther than the naked eye allows. While it can increase gains, it also exposes you to greater risk. Careful analysis and risk management are essential when employing leverage.

105) "The use of leverage can significantly enhance returns when managed properly."

— Ray Dalio

Ray Dalio, a billionaire hedge fund manager, emphasizes that leverage can boost returns if handled correctly. It's like driving a high-performance car; in the right hands, it excels, but without skill, it can be dangerous. Implementing strict controls and diversifying investments can mitigate risks associated with leverage.

106) "Good debt helps you get richer; bad debt makes you poorer."

— Robert Kiyosaki

Robert Kiyosaki reiterates the importance of distinguishing between good and bad debt. Good debt is an investment in your future income, like a mortgage on a rental property. Bad debt drains resources, like credit card debt for non-essential items. Recognizing this difference guides you toward financial decisions that build wealth rather than diminish it.

107) "Debt can obscure the true fragility of a system, creating an illusion of stability while hiding underlying vulnerabilities."

— Nassim Taleb

Nassim Taleb's quote cuts to the heart of how debt can trick us into thinking things are more stable than they really are. It's like putting a fresh coat of paint over a crumbling wall—everything looks fine on the surface, but underneath, there's real fragility. Debt can mask the weaknesses in a system, whether it's a business, a government, or even personal finances, giving the illusion of strength and stability. But when pressure hits, those hidden vulnerabilities come crashing down. The key lesson here? Don't be fooled by the appearance of stability fueled by debt. True strength comes from a solid foundation, not from borrowing to cover up cracks. Recognize the risks and address them before the illusion shatters.

108) "Excessive government debt can lead to economic instability and place a heavy burden on future generations. Fiscal responsibility is essential for sustainable economic growth."

— Thomas Sowell

Thomas Sowell's quote serves as a wake-up call about the long-term dangers of excessive government debt. It's like running up a massive credit card bill, but instead of just dealing with it yourself, you're passing it down to your kids and grandkids. Too much debt can make the economy wobbly and unpredictable, leading to higher taxes, reduced services, or even economic crises. Sowell's message is simple: fiscal responsibility is key to keeping things stable and ensuring future generations aren't left holding the bag. The value here? Just like in personal finance, a balanced budget is the foundation for sustainable growth—because no one wants to inherit a mountain of debt and instability.

109) "The less debt you carry, the greater your personal freedom and peace of mind."

— Naval Ravikant

Naval Ravikant's quote hits on a simple truth: the less debt you have, the more freedom you gain. It's like shedding a heavy backpack on a long hike. Suddenly, every step feels lighter, and the path ahead becomes easier. Debt can weigh you down, limiting your choices and creating constant worry. Without it, you have more control over your life, time, and decisions. The message here is powerful: reducing debt isn't just about numbers on a balance sheet, it's about reclaiming your peace of mind and living with the kind of freedom that lets you focus on what truly matters.

110) "The use of leverage requires discipline and a deep understanding of risk."

— Financial Insight

Leverage, in its essence, is not just a tool for amplifying gains but a finely sharpened weapon that, in the wrong hands, cuts deeper than anticipated. The promise of reward tempts you to lean forward, yet only the disciplined maintain their balance. The uninitiated are seduced by the allure of quick returns, blind to the precariousness of their position. The true master, however, understands that leverage magnifies wealth and risk. It is a delicate game of control, where foresight and strategy must reign supreme. Seek wisdom and expert counsel as one seeks a map before traversing a dangerous landscape. To grasp leverage without fully understanding its intricacies is to court disaster, but to wield it with precision is to command forces others dare not touch.

111) "To create antifragile systems, it's essential to minimize unnecessary debt and avoid excessive leverage, thereby reducing potential points of failure."

— Nassim Taleb

To create antifragile systems, you must first recognize that debt is a silent predator, waiting for the slightest misstep to pounce. Debt adds fragility, exposing you to forces beyond your control. Leverage, while tempting, is nothing more than a mirage of power. It gives you the illusion of strength while quietly planting the seeds of your downfall. Nassim Taleb warns against this trap. The true strategist minimizes exposure, ensuring their system survives and thrives amid chaos. When you eliminate unnecessary debt, you strip away the vulnerabilities that others succumb to. In this, you attain a form of invincibility, prepared for disruption, immune to collapse, and always one step ahead of those trapped in their self-made web of liabilities. Master your risks, or be mastered by them.

112) "Debt is a claim upon future earnings, a deduction from future spending."

— George Gissing

George Gissing points out that debt reduces our future income. It's like signing over a portion of your paycheck before you earn it. Recognizing this helps us understand the long-term impact of debt on our financial freedom and encourages cautious borrowing. By minimizing debt, you retain more of your future earnings for yourself, allowing greater flexibility and the ability to pursue your goals.

113) *"Those who understand interest earn it; those who don't, pay it."*

— Albert Einstein

Einstein masterfully captures the divide between financial wisdom and ignorance. If you understand how interest works, you can harness it to grow your wealth through smart investments and savings. But if you don't, interest becomes a relentless opponent, eating away at your resources through credit card debt or high-interest loans. By learning the rules of interest, you can turn it from a financial drain into a powerful tool that works for you, not against you.

114) "Out of debt, out of danger."

— English Proverb

Without the burden of debt, you can navigate life with far less risk and uncertainty. When you're free from owing money, you're better equipped to face unexpected challenges, whether a surprise expense or an unforeseen opportunity. Debt often acts like an anchor, dragging you into stress and limiting your choices. On the other hand, financial stability allows for peace of mind, giving you the freedom to move through life with confidence, knowing you're not vulnerable to the dangers of owing others. In modern life, you can often throw money at problems until they disappear. It is hard to be in danger when you are not in debt.

115) "Debt is like a fire—it can either cook your food or burn your house down. "

— Traditional Proverb

This proverb compares debt to fire, a tool that can be helpful or destructive. Managed wisely, debt can enable growth; mismanagement can cause ruin. The key lies in careful handling.

116) "Excessive debt within financial systems can lead to catastrophic failures, as small disturbances may trigger widespread instability. "

— Nassim Taleb

Nassim Taleb's quote warns us about the ticking time bomb of excessive debt in financial systems. It's like stacking a house of cards. Everything looks fine until the straw that breaks the camel's back knocks it all down. In a system overloaded with debt, even a small disruption can cause a ripple effect, leading to widespread chaos and collapse, known as contagion. When debt builds up too high, the whole system is fragile and vulnerable to sudden, catastrophic failures. The key is to keep the structure strong by limiting debt so small problems don't snowball into full-blown crises. Always have liquidity available when the inevitable collapse comes.

117) "Change is painful. Few people have the courage to seek out change."

— Dave Ramsey

Dave Ramsey's quote reminds us that change is tough, and most people would rather avoid it than face the discomfort head-on. It's like stepping into cold water; you know it's going to be uncomfortable at first, but once you take the plunge, you realize it's not as bad as anticipated. Ramsey's point? Change, especially when it comes to finances or personal growth, requires courage because it often involves facing painfully hard truths and struggling to break bad habits. The change may be painful in the short term, but it's the key to long-term progress. Only those brave enough to embrace it will reap the rewards on the other side.

118) *"Debt is a prolific mother of folly and crime."*

— Benjamin Disraeli

Disraeli shines a harsh light on the cascading effects of debt. It's as if debt gives birth to a series of unfortunate offspring, poor decisions, desperation, and sometimes even illegal actions. When financial pressure builds, people may be tempted into unwise shortcuts or risky schemes to stay afloat, creating a slippery slope where one misstep leads to another. Disraeli's words remind us that staying out of excessive debt is not just about protecting our wallets but also safeguarding our integrity and decision-making. By avoiding debt traps, we can steer clear of the temptations that often arise from financial desperation and maintain a path of sound judgment and ethical choices.

119) *"Debt is a trap which man sets and baits himself, and then deliberately gets into."*

— Josh Billings (Henry Wheeler Shaw)

Billings humorously points out how we often become our own worst enemy when it comes to finances. It's like laying out a trap, sprinkling the bait of instant gratification. Whether it's a new gadget, vacation, or luxury, we walk right into it often with full awareness of the consequences. By recognizing this self-sabotage, we gain the power to step back, rethink our choices, and avoid falling into the debt cycle. Practicing discipline and mindful spending keeps us from setting traps we'll later regret, freeing us from the snare of unnecessary debt.

120) "Personal debt limits individual resilience and flexibility, while societal debt can constrain collective adaptability in the face of unforeseen events."

— Nassim Taleb

Nassim Taleb's quote paints a clear picture of how debt can tie both individuals and societies into troublesome knots. On a personal level, carrying too much debt feels like being stuck in quicksand; every move becomes harder, and your ability to bounce back from life's surprises shrinks. On a larger scale, societal debt is like a ball and chain that drags down a nation's ability to adapt when crises hit. Whether it's an individual or an entire society, too much debt means less flexibility and resilience in the face of the unexpected. The takeaway? Keeping debt in check is crucial to staying nimble and robust, ready to handle whatever life, or the world, throws your way.

121) "Money borrowed is soon sorrowed."

— Traditional Proverb

Debt can quickly turn from a temporary solution into a source of regret. It's like indulging in a rich dessert that later causes a stomachache. You enjoy the moment, but the consequences linger. Borrowing may seem like a quick fix, but the burden of repayment, often with added interest, can weigh heavily on your future. The proverb urges us to think carefully before taking on debt, reminding us that short-term relief can lead to long-term discomfort.

122) "Using debt wisely can be a tool for growth, but it's essential to understand the risks and manage it carefully."

— Naval Ravikant

Naval Ravikant's quote highlights the double-edged nature of debt. It can be a powerful tool for growth, but only if you handle it with care. Think of debt like fire: it can warm your home and cook your meals, but if left unchecked, it can burn everything down. The message here is that debt can help you expand and achieve more than you could by relying only on your capital when used wisely. However, it's crucial to fully understand the risks and keep them under control because if mismanaged, it can quickly spiral into a burden. The value? Debt can fuel success, but only if you respect its power and never let it get out of hand.

123) "A good payer is master of another's purse."

— Scottish Proverb

Those who settle their debts promptly wield influence far beyond their own finances. It's like being the trusted friend who always returns borrowed tools on time. You'll likely be the first to get help when you need it again. By paying on time, you build credibility and trust, making others more willing to lend to you, extend credit, or even offer better terms. Essentially, responsible payers unlock the power of other people's resources, turning financial reliability into an asset of its own. The incentive of the lender is always to lend to the person who poses the least amount of risk. Ensure the lender knows that the person is you.

124) *"A poor man who owes nothing is rich."*

— Traditional Proverb

True wealth isn't about fancy possessions but about freedom from debt. Imagine living in a small, cozy house that's fully yours versus being trapped in a mansion with endless mortgage payments hanging over your head. The absence of debt brings a sense of financial peace and independence that money can't always buy. It's a reminder that wealth isn't just about what you have, but also about what you don't owe, freedom from debt is like owning a quiet treasure that brings lasting security and well-being.

125) "He who buys what he does not need steals from himself."

— Swedish Proverb

This proverb serves as a clever reminder of the hidden cost of unnecessary spending. It's like robbing your future self of opportunities, as each impulse buy chips away at resources that could be invested in something more meaningful. By practicing mindful spending, you protect your financial well-being, ensuring that your money works for you rather than disappearing into things that offer fleeting satisfaction. It's a call to align your purchases with your true needs and goals, preserving wealth for what truly matters. Will your future self be better or worse off after a purchase? Answering that question will provide a sound filter for spending decisions.

126) "Debt is the worst kind of poverty because it robs you of your future earnings."

— Financial Insight

Debt chains your future to the past, making you work tomorrow for what you've already spent. Debt isn't just a financial burden in the present; it takes from your future earnings and limits your ability to save, invest, or seize new opportunities due to the servicing of interest. It can be like running on a treadmill where, no matter how hard you work, you're not moving forward because yesterday's expenses are dragging you back. Eliminating debt frees you from that cycle, allowing you to use your income for growth, dreams, and financial freedom instead of playing catch-up. Debt may feel like a quick fix, but in the long run, it's the heaviest kind of poverty.

127) "Don't let the fear of losing be greater than the excitement of winning."

— Robert Kiyosaki

Don't let the fear of rain stop you from planting seeds. Otherwise, you'll never have a harvest. It's a reminder that if you're too scared of losing, you might miss out on big wins. In the world of finances, this means taking smart, calculated risks rather than playing it too safe out of fear. Sure, there's always the chance things won't go as planned, but if you never invest or try, you'll also never see the rewards. Just make sure your risks are informed so you're not gambling recklessly or diving into debt. Balance your excitement with caution, and you'll be ready to seize opportunities while avoiding financial pitfalls. Manage the investing budget!

128) *"A budget is telling your money where to go instead of wondering where it went."*

— Dave Ramsey

Dave Ramsey's quote makes budgeting sound like the ultimate power move. It's about being the boss of your money instead of letting it run wild. Think of a budget as a roadmap: when you tell your money where to go, every dollar has a purpose, and you stay in control. Knowledge is power, and a budget is simply the knowledge of where your money is going. This knowledge allows you to get power over your money. Without a budget, you're left scratching your head at the end of the month, wondering where all your hard-earned cash disappeared. The key takeaway? A budget isn't restrictive; it's empowering. It lets you direct your finances with intention so that you're in charge of your money, not the other way around.

129) "In the long run, we shape our lives, and we shape ourselves."

— Eleanor Roosevelt

You're the artist of your own life, and every decision you make is a stroke of the chisel. In the long run, the habits and choices we make, whether about money, health, or relationships, are what shape who we become. Just like a sculptor carefully carves out a statue, the financial decisions you make today, from saving to borrowing, are shaping the foundation of your future. If you're mindful about spending and debt, you're sculpting a life of stability and freedom. If not, you might find cracks in the statue later. In the end, you create the life you live through your choices, so be intentional with every move.

130) *"Cut your coat according to your cloth."*

— English Proverb

Don't design a mansion when you've only got a cottage's worth of bricks! This English proverb reminds us to live within our means, tailoring our lifestyle to fit what we actually have, not what we wish we had. By managing expenses to match your income, you avoid the temptation of overspending and the trap of debt. It's all about making smart, realistic choices so you don't end up with financial stress. Just like a perfectly fitted coat, living within your means ensures comfort and balance, allowing you to build wealth steadily without stretching yourself too thin. Never, ever, spend in the hopes of impressing your neighbours. They won't notice, and it will only hurt your financial circumstances.

131) "When you borrow trouble, you give your peace away."

— Traditional Saying

This traditional saying is like a gentle reminder that borrowing trouble, whether it's unnecessary debt or needless stress, is the quickest way to rob yourself of peace. Things were steady until you invited the chaos. Taking on burdens that you don't need, like piling up debt or overcommitting to stressful obligations, only disrupts your inner calm. Protecting your peace means being mindful of what you allow into your life, saying "no" to things that bring more worry than benefit, and focusing on what truly adds value without compromising your well-being. Peace is priceless; don't trade it away.

132) *"Building wealth is not just about increasing income, but also about reducing liabilities and avoiding unnecessary debt."*

— Naval Ravikant

Sure, making more money is great, but if you're constantly losing it to debt and liabilities, you're not really building wealth. You're just patching leaks. True wealth isn't just about how much you make; it's about how much you keep. Reducing liabilities, like cutting down on debt and avoiding unnecessary expenses, is just as important as increasing your income. By plugging the holes and keeping your financial foundation strong, you set yourself up for lasting wealth, not just a temporary boost.

133) *"Time is money."*

— Benjamin Franklin

Every hour has a price tag on it, whether you're making money or letting it slip through your fingers. Time, just like cash, is a limited resource, and how you spend it directly impacts your financial success. If you waste time, you're essentially throwing money out the window. On the flip side, managing your time efficiently can lead to greater earnings and opportunities. The same goes for debt: procrastinating on repayments only makes the interest pile up, costing you more in the long run. Treat your time like money, and you'll make smarter, wealth-building decisions. Have you defined an hourly rate for your time? I recommend doing so immediately.

134) "Don't dig your grave with your own knife and fork."

— English Proverb

This English proverb is a perfect reminder that sometimes we're our own worst enemy. Whether it's health or money, the tools of destruction are often in our own hands. When it comes to finances, overspending and piling up debt is like digging your own financial grave with every swipe of the credit card. Just as too much indulgence can hurt your body, reckless spending can wreak havoc on your financial well-being. The key is moderation: living within your means, budgeting wisely, and saving for the future. That way, you're building wealth instead of a debt-filled hole you'll struggle to climb out of!

135) "Taking responsibility for your financial decisions, including how you handle debt, is crucial for long-term success."

— Naval Ravikant

You're the captain of your financial ship. Don't blame the storm if you've got the wheel. Taking responsibility for your money decisions, especially managing debt, means acknowledging that your financial future is yours. It's not about getting lucky or hoping things will magically improve; it's about making thoughtful choices that steer you toward long-term success. Whether you're paying down debt or planning for the future, taking ownership gives you the power to course-correct and build the life you want. Responsibility isn't a burden. It's the key to financial freedom and by far the best life strategy.

136) *"An ounce of prevention is worth a pound of cure."*

— Benjamin Franklin

A little effort today can save you a mountain of trouble down the road. Whether it's about health, finances, or life in general, taking small preventative steps, like saving for emergencies, maintaining healthy habits, or planning ahead, can keep you from dealing with much bigger, costlier problems later. It's way easier (and cheaper!) to handle a tiny crack now than to deal with a flood later. In other words, prevention is the ultimate life hack for avoiding future disasters!

137) *"You must gain control over your money, or the lack of it will forever control you. "*

— Dave Ramsey

Either you take charge of your money, or it's going to boss you around for life! Imagine your finances as a wild horse: if you don't grab the reins and guide it, you'll be dragged through the mud of debt, stress, and poor choices. Gaining control means making a plan and sticking to it, so you're in charge of where your money goes instead of wondering where it all went. When you manage your money, you should have a plan for every dollar. You're steering your financial ship toward security and freedom rather than letting the winds of poor decisions blow you off course!

138) *"Financial peace isn't the acquisition of stuff. It's learning to live on less than you make."*

— Dave Ramsey

Dave Ramsey's quote is like saying happiness isn't in the shiny new car or the latest gadget—it's in knowing you've got control over your money, not the other way around. Financial peace means you're not constantly playing catch-up or stressing about bills. It's about being content with what you have rather than chasing more stuff that often only leads to anxiety or debt. When you master this mindset, you free up income to save, invest, and give generously, creating a life where your finances bring peace instead of pressure. It's like trading the thrill of the moment for long-term security, a trade worth making at any time.

139) "Do not save what is left after spending; instead, spend what is left after saving."

— Warren Buffett

Warren Buffett's advice is like telling you to eat your veggies before diving into dessert! He's flipping the usual mindset of spending first and saving whatever's left (which, let's be honest, often isn't much). Instead, saving before you even think about spending guarantees your financial pantry is stocked for the future. It's like paying your future self first and forcing your present self to be more mindful of what's left. That way, you build up savings without feeling deprived, and you avoid the trap of lifestyle inflation. After all, true financial freedom is sweeter than any impulse buy!

140) "Compound interest is the eighth wonder of the world. He who understands it earns it; he who doesn't, pays it."

— Albert Einstein

Einstein wasn't kidding when he called compound interest the eighth wonder of the world. Its financial magic in action! Picture a snowball rolling downhill, picking up more snow as it goes, getting bigger and bigger. That's what happens when your money starts earning interest, and then that interest earns even more interest. Over time, small investments grow into a mountain of wealth. The trick? Start early and be patient. On the flip side, if you don't understand it, compound interest can work against you in debt, where you're the one paying that ever-growing snowball. Master it, and you've got a powerful tool that will lead to financial freedom.

141) "The only way you will ever permanently take control of your financial life is to dig deep and fix the root problem."

— Suze Orman

Suze Orman hits the nail on the head when she says you've got to dig deep to fix the root of your financial problems. It's like trying to fix a leaky roof by just mopping up the puddles. Until you fix the actual leak, the problem keeps coming back! The same goes for money: if you're constantly in debt or can't save, the real issue might not be overspending but how you think about money, your habits, your emotional dysregulation, or your financial education. Maybe it's emotional spending, ignoring budgets, or not knowing where your money goes. Fix the core issue, and you'll stop the leaks, giving yourself the foundation to build real financial control!

142) *"Financial freedom is available to those who learn about it and work for it."*

— Robert Kiyosaki

Achieving financial freedom is like mastering a craft. It's a mix of learning, practice, and discipline. Robert Kiyosaki reminds us that the door to financial independence doesn't magically open; it requires you to pick up financial literacy tools and work diligently toward this goal. It means educating yourself about saving, investing, and managing money wisely while actively applying those lessons to your life. Just like a sculptor shapes a masterpiece with every chip, your consistent efforts, whether it's budgeting, investing, or building passive income streams, carve the path toward the freedom to live life on your own terms.

143) "When governments accumulate large debts, they often have to offer higher interest rates to attract investors, which can crowd out private investment and hinder economic expansion."

— Thomas Sowell

Thomas Sowell's quote highlights the domino effect that government debt can trigger. When a government racks up massive debt, it often needs to offer higher interest rates to combat the inevitable inflation. But here's the catch: when those higher rates grab all the investible capital, it crowds out private businesses trying to raise money for growth. It's like the government hogging all the oxygen, leaving less for everyone else. This shift can choke off opportunities for private companies to expand, which in turn slows down overall economic growth. The takeaway? When governments let debt spiral out of control, it's not just their problem—it impacts the entire economy by limiting the space for private investment to flourish.

144) "Living beyond one's means through excessive borrowing is unsustainable and leads to long-term financial problems, whether at the personal or national level."

— Thomas Sowell

Thomas Sowell's quote clearly warns about the dangers of living beyond your means. It's like running on a treadmill that keeps speeding up, you might keep going for a while, but eventually, you're going to trip and fall. Whether it's personal debt or a nation running indefinite deficits, borrowing more than you can handle isn't sustainable. It leads to a future filled with financial headaches, from mounting interest to limited optionality. The message? Borrowing may seem like a quick fix, but without restraint, it becomes a trap. Long-term stability comes from living within your means and running a surplus today so you don't face bigger problems down the road.

145) "Debt is normal. Be weird."

— Dave Ramsey

Dave Ramsey's quote flips the script on how we think about debt. In a world where debt has become the norm, credit cards, car loans, and mortgages, it's easy to follow the crowd. But Ramsey's challenge is to "be weird" by breaking away from that cycle. It's like walking in the opposite direction on a moving sidewalk: Sure, it takes effort, but you're heading toward freedom while everyone else is just going with the flow. The value here? Being "weird" by avoiding debt and living below your means isn't just a quirky choice—it's a smart strategy for building financial freedom and peace of mind. After all, when ordinary means being in debt, weird is the new wealthy.

146) "The wise man bridges the gap by laying out the path by means of which he can get from where he is to where he wants to go."

— J.P. Morgan

Whether it's crushing debt or stacking wealth, success doesn't come from wishful thinking, it comes from laying down a step-by-step plan that takes you from Point A to Point Financial Freedom. Think of it as constructing a bridge over the gap between your current situation and your goals. Each plank is a small, strategic action: budgeting smarter, saving consistently, or investing wisely. Before you know it, that chasm of "how will I ever get there?" becomes a sturdy path toward your bright financial future!

147) "You can't get out of debt while keeping the same lifestyle that got you there."

— Dave Ramsey

Getting out of debt while keeping the same lifestyle is like trying to lose weight while devouring pizza every night! If you're living the same way that got you into the financial hole, you're just digging it deeper. To climb out, you've got to make changes: cut back on unnecessary expenses, skip the impulse buys, and channel that extra cash into paying down what you owe. It's about swapping short-term pleasures for long-term financial freedom. Remember, a few sacrifices today could mean living debt-free and stress-free tomorrow. The pizza can wait!

148) "An investment in knowledge pays the best interest."

— Benjamin Franklin

Investing in knowledge is like planting a money tree that keeps giving. Only this tree grows inside your brain! While stocks can crash and real estate bubbles burst, the wisdom you gain from learning never devalues. Whether it's mastering a new skill or leveling up your financial IQ, knowledge compounds over time, allowing you to make smarter decisions and avoid costly mistakes. It's the gift that keeps on giving, letting you navigate life's money maze with a map instead of blindly bumping into walls. In short, the more you know, the more you grow, both mentally and financially!

149) "He who is quick to borrow is slow to pay."

— German Proverb

Watch out for the person who borrows money faster than you can say "loan shark." they're usually the ones who disappear when it's time to settle up. Some telltale signs? They dodge talking about finances, always have a new excuse ("The bank messed up my transfer!" or "I'll pay you next Friday for sure!"), and suddenly become Houdini when repayment day arrives. If their spending habits seem flashy but their promises feel shaky, you might end up playing hide-and-seek with your cash. As the proverb suggests, fast borrowing often means slow, if any, paying, so lend with caution!

150) "The art is not in making money but in keeping it."

— Proverb

Keeping money is like holding onto water—it's slippery unless you have the right container! To keep it from leaking away, you need to plug the common holes: impulsive spending, lifestyle inflation, and poor investment choices. Set clear financial goals, automate savings, and invest in appreciating assets that grow your wealth while you sleep. Just as important, track your spending like a detective and adjust when things get off track. Remember, anyone can make money, but the real skill lies in protecting it from your own bad habits.

www.ingramcontent.com/pod-product-compliance
Lightning Source LLC
Chambersburg PA
CBHW071504220526
45472CB00003B/914